ALONg
the
BuMPY
ROAD

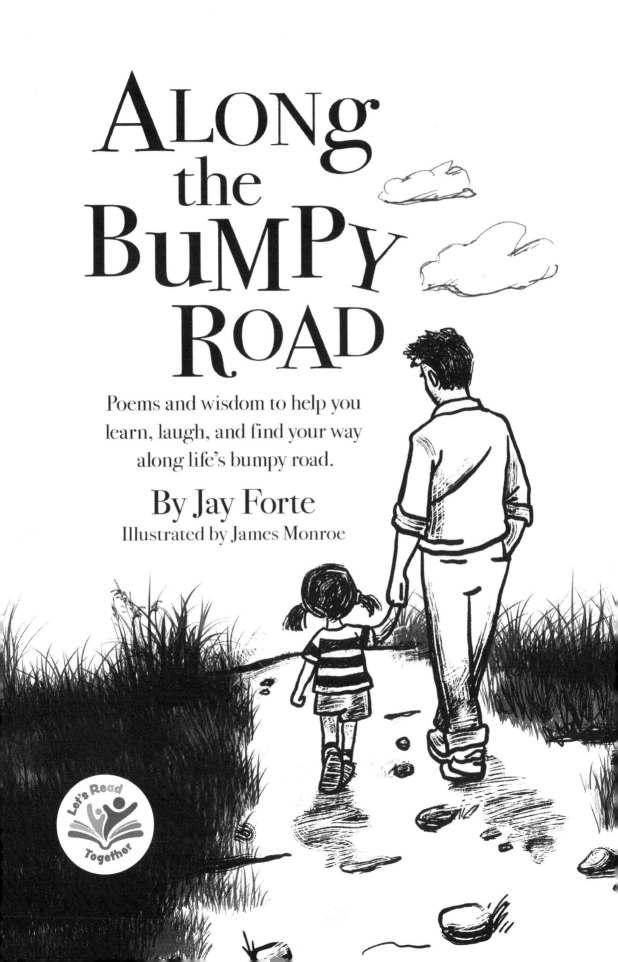

Along the Bumpy Road

Poems and wisdom to help you learn, laugh, and find your way along life's bumpy road.

By Jay Forte
Illustrated by James Monroe

Let's Read Together

Illustrated by James Monroe.
Cover and interior design by JamesMonroeDesign.com.

Softcover ISBN: 978-1-7350214-5-4
Hardcover ISBN: 978-1-7350214-4-7

Printed in the United States of America
First Printing: 2024
28 27 26 25 24   5 4 3 2 1

 The Greatness Zone
thegreatnesszone.com

In partnership with Wisdom/Work

For my family and other life guides
who share with me how to navigate life's bumps.

Contents

Learn from Your World

To Laugh and Have Fun

Introduction

Life is a bumpy road. It has highs, it has lows. It has adventures and challenges. Some things work out. Some things don't. Sometimes we laugh, sometimes we cry. The bumps are just part of life.

Along the Bumpy Road shares practical life wisdom through poems to help all of us meet life's bumps with patience and grace, embrace who we are, learn from our world and make time for fun—to have great and amazing lives.

As part of the **Let's Read Together** book series, this poetry collection encourages reading time together away from technology. In these special read-together moments, and prompted by questions and characters in many of the poems, you have the space to dream, invent, share ideas, understand yourself and others, and develop stronger relationships.

To be read alone or aloud, to your kids, for yourself, as a family or in a classroom, **Along the Bumpy Road** has content for all ages.

May the rhymes entertain you, the characters inspire you and the wisdom guide you.

Travel wisely and well along life's bumpy road.

Jay Forte

Dealing With Bumps

Along the Bumpy Road

Life's road can be bumpy, that's just how it is,
Some highs and some lows, some smooth and some fizz.
Some things work out and some not at all,
Sometimes you feel great and sometimes you feel small.

Life sends us successes to help us go cheer!
Life sends us the challenge to manage our fear.
Life sends some highs to help us feel fine,
Life sends some lows so we learn to be kind.

Life sends us winning and times of success,
To amp up the juice and help us feel blessed.
Then life sends the failures and times that we lose,
They teach us key lessons, if we heed its big news.

The bumps are a pain, we don't like them at all,
Like when some of your friends don't make time to call.
Or when you're embarrassed by something you say,
Or when you show up on a completely wrong day.

Along the Bumpy Road

The bumps are only one **small** part of life,
I know they feel big and loaded with strife.
But bumps are a gift, they've something to share,
They can make your life better, when you meet them with care.

If you're mad or sad when things don't go your way,
Ask, "Why should I waste this wonderful day?"
You know that the bumps come along on the ride,
Whenever they happen, it shows you're alive.

Don't stop when you're down or even when mad,
Take a deep breath, think it through and act glad.
Disappointments are lessons about something brand new,
They can **really** help make the **very** best you.

So read through this book, so calm you will stay
Through life's little bumps that are coming your way.
Learn **how** to meet them, grow and don't hide,
The bumps make your life a great wild ride.

Dealing With Bumps

When It's Just Not Your Day

I knew it first thing, when I started the day
That things would not **go** in my way.
I tried to be happy and grateful, I say.
But I already knew, it was just not my day.

I tripped on the stairs and came down with a crash.
I dropped my dad's phone in the sink with a splash.
The note for my teacher got thrown in the trash.
This day, I just knew, would not be a fun dash.

At school, my teacher focused on me.
Telling and scolding is all I did see.
"Start over! Be quiet! Stand in line!" said she.
Today is not great, I bet you agree.

I missed the bus and walked home in the rain.
I stepped off the curb, gave my ankle a sprain.
I got soaked with the spray from a car in the lane.
Today, you can see, is a very big pain.

When It's Just Not Your Day

Home and all wet, to my room with a huff.
I needed a moment when feeling this gruff.
Things that had happened were **so** truly tough.
Today, on this day, I had **just** had enough.

Then to the kitchen, head in my hands,
Upset at a day I did **not** understand.
How things can go against **all** of my plans.
Today, was the **worst** day in all of the land.

Mom asked, "What's up, what's making you sad?"
"Nothing," I said, trying not to get mad.
"Tell me," she said, "of the day that you had.
Can we make it much better, or a little less bad?"

I shrugged then recounted without a delay,
How everything seemed to **not** go my way.
Not sure what could help or what thing she could say,
That still might improve this most horrible day.

She smiled and said, "Some days make you scream.
They feel like an awful and really bad dream.
There's **one** thing that makes it a bit less extreme,
A very big bowl of your favorite ice cream."

Two scoops and my mood changed, right on the spot.
We talked about stuff and what the day brought.
Some things work out and others do not,
Life sends what it sends, you get what you got.

"I'll smile and keep moving," to yourself you should say,
When you find there are things that do **not** go your way.
Some moments are bright, and others are gray,
Don't let **anything** stop you from loving your day.

How do you handle things that don't go your way?

Weird Words

You say the wrong things or an error you make.
You're not alone, we **all** make mistakes.
And our tempers start climbing, we get **super** mad,
And sometimes that makes us act out **real** bad.

What we need is something to do or to say,
To focus our feelings in a **much** better way.
For that I like words, the strange and weird ones,
To shift out of anger and get back to some fun.

Here are some words I made up and I like,
When I want my anger to **go take a hike**;

I say, **buffa, snarfa** or **yellow-blue binky**,
Hoffa, tartuffa or **huffy green stinky**.
I say **snarka, moolina** and **gully wonkino**,
Parlata, namulli or **huffy starino**.

Weird words are great, they make me laugh,
They get rid of the grumpies with a wave of a staff.
I just can't stay angry when I use these weird words,
My anger goes up to the sky with the birds.

So, what did **you** think of? What words will **you** use,
When you're angry or mad or are feeling the blues?
Write them down to use them when the time is just right,
Have them to help make your anger take flight.

Weird words can help when your anger is high,
They send off bad feelings, to go and fly by.
They'll make you feel better, you just have to say,
Your goofy weird words for a much better day.

What are some weird words you could use?

Hoft and Sard

Some people are pushy and talk way too loud,
Their voices seem to take over the crowd.
They like to take charge, they act like the boss,
When you don't **do** as they say, they get truly cross.

Other people, you'll see, are gentle and kind,
Not a bad word or problem they'll find.
They never do challenge or even push back,
They are happy to take a more friendly tack.

Dealing With Bumps

Too hard—not for me, don't like that at all.
Too soft—not much better, always taking the fall.
Someplace in between is the best way to be,
To say what you need, but to say it kindly.

Change the H to an S and a new word is **Sard**,
That's adding some kindness to soften the word **hard**.
Change the S to an H and make the word **Hoft**,
That's adding some strength to toughen the word **soft**.

Not too hard, not too soft, that's just how to be,
Say what you need, but do it kindly.
Be hard and determined about things that can matter,
Be soft and care deeply and no heart you will shatter.

Try Hoft and Sard, we made them, they're new.
Go use them, go try them, that's something to do.
If you're soft, then get stronger by just a small bit,
If your hard then go softer, go try it, don't quit.

Try out these new words, and I bet you will find,
That your days will be good and a whole lot more kind.
These words will remind you to show better care,
That's how to be great in the world that we share.

How can you be more Sard? How can you be more Hoft?

Let Off Some Steam

There will be times, you know this is true,
When the things that happen can aggravate you.
Anger, frustration, disappointments arrive,
And you feel like you're stung by bees from a hive.

That's normal to have all these feelings, you know.
They confuse you about which way you should go.
Feel them, you must, that's what we all do,
But don't let them linger, they'll really hurt you.

So, what you need when things are real tough,
Is to let off some steam without being rough.
A word, a phrase to manage emotion,
Can help you move on without too much commotion.

Dealing With Bumps

Say Grrr! or Shazzam! or another fun word,
To release the hot feelings to the sky like a bird.
Or grit your teeth, make a fist or just scream.
These help you release so much of your steam.

Try out some ways to vent and move on,
Don't stay **hurt** or **mad** till the day is all gone.
Feel it, release it, then move on with your day.
Life is much better when you live in this way.

What are some ways you can let off some steam and move on?

13

Grumpy Be Gone

I woke up a Grumpy, I'm just not sure why,
I didn't have reason to be.
I wanted to wake as sweet as plum pie,
But I woke up a big Grumpy me.

"Snap out of it," said Mom, "make it go bye,
This is not how to get on with your day.
Think for a bit of some things you can try,
To send that big Grumpy away."

So I picture my Grumpy as lumpy and green,
With boogers, farts, and more.
That's just not the way I want to be seen,
So I kicked him right out of my door.

My smile comes back, the Grumpy is gone,
My day is now just the best.
I watch as the Grumpy moves out past my lawn,
Going somewhere to make a new mess.

What do you do to get rid of your grumpies?

Dealing With Bumps

Be Yourself

Superhero

Yes, that's **you**, a superhero you are,
No need for a cape or to fly very far.
There's things about you, so special are they,
That make you **so super**, I just have to say.

It could be the way you're so great with art,
Or that you're kind and have a big heart.

It could be the way you can figure things out,
Or control your temper with no need to shout.

It could be the way that you lead with your smile,
Or that you do things with really great style.

It could be the way you can play any sport,
Or that you know how to build a snow fort.

It could be the way you're a big help at home,
Or that you never get lost when you go out to roam.

It could be the way you are there for your friends,
Or that you control the money you spend.

It could be the way you tell a great story,
Or let others take credit and feel all the glory.

Be Yourself

It could be the way you are ready to share,
Or that you know the right things to wear.

It could be the way you grow things and cook,
Or that you love to spend time with great books.

A superhero, that's YOU! I hope you agree,
And notice the same, a superhero, that's ME!

We each have our things, unique like our face,
We can make our world a much better place.

So, take a long moment, look deep deep inside,
What makes you so great? What makes you feel pride?

Down deep you are great in **so** many ways,
So, bring something great to each of your days.

How will you be a superhero today?

The Real Me

"Hmm," I thought as the teacher asked about **me**,
To say something clever, there just had to be.

Should I say my dad runs a rich fancy store?
Or I was raised in Alaska, on a mountain or shore?
Should I say I am older than my young looks give way?
Or I have many pets I can't leave for one day?

Should I wow her with showing how smart that I am,
That I can cook, or braise, or roast a fresh ham?
I could say I speak Russian, Spanish or Greek,
Or can memorize a book with simply a peek.

Be Yourself

I could say I'm royalty—my dad is a king,
That I have my own crown, my scepter and ring.
I could say, at my age, a jet I can fly,
Or that I can do **anything** if I give it a try.

I could say I'm rich and clever and smart.
I am popular, and witty and amazing with art.
I could say I dance, write, sing and can build,
Or can name all the titles in a bookstore so filled.

Should I say that I know all the parts of a car?
Or that my traveling always takes me afar,
To Bombay and Lisbon, Paris and Rome?
Or, I'm someone who has more than one home?

I could say I have three much older sisters,
Or can walk on hot coals and never get blisters.
I could say a homerun I always can hit,
Or, when things get tough, I'm not one to quit.

She is waiting for me to share some good news,
About who that I am; I'll just have to choose.
So, what do I say? Many things it could be.
But I know the right answer should be the **real** me.

So what will I say? I got it. I know.
I'll be honest—I like travel and watching things grow.
I like soccer, baseball and fun family time,
But my most favorite thing is making words rhyme.

What would you say when some asks about you?

What If?

What if I were a lizard with a really long nose?
What if I were a cat with fifteen wide toes?
What if I were a horse with the brightest white mane?
What if I had a brother who would never complain?

What if I could eat pancakes, 100 at once?
What if I could do the most amazing of stunts?
What if I could dance on my feet and my head?
What if I could bake sharp, pointy blue bread?

What if I could fly without any wings?
What if I could remember hundreds of things?
What if I could speak French, Dutch or Greek?
What if I could learn things with just a small peek?

What if I could swim like an enormous white shark?
What if I could sing like the lark in the park?
What if I were 9 feet when I stand in my socks?
What If I could eat wood and stones and rocks?

I like to imagine the weird things Dad said.
I like to invent things right out of my head.
I like to ask **What if?** and **How About?**
They make my mind work; ideas just fall out.

**It's your turn to dream, invent and to go,
Start with 'What if I could?' and let your thoughts flow.**

Guiding the Way

My mom says I'm talented and gifted and blessed,
That has nothing to do with my grades on a test.
It's about who I am and who I will be,
And making the world **better** by just being **me**.

Sure, sometimes that means Mom needs to scold,
As I act immature and not at all old.
"But that's how you grow," she says with a smile.
"And growing can sometimes take a great while."

Be Yourself

We all have to do it, it's how we get wise,
It's how that we learn to live and decide
Who we should be and **what** things do matter,
To be our best selves and avoid all the chatter.

Each day of our life is just part of our trip,
Life's an adventure with rises and dips.
Some highs and some lows, like mountains and valleys,
Down main streets and back roads and even some alleys.

Each road is all new with **great** things to see.
Each adventure can show how **strong** we can be.
Each moment reminds us to love this great ride,
Go out and live bold, there's no reason to hide.

To move to the future, a place all unknown,
I'll need some help so I'm never alone.
For those who love me will serve as my guides,
To support and encourage, so I'll take my great strides.

Get up and get moving, there are things to get done.
There is work and some school, but a whole lot of fun.
Trust there are some who will watch and help steer,
I know in each day I have **nothing** to fear.

They say, "Go out and be **great**, don't worry or fret.
Go out and be brave, don't hold back or regret.
We're here to encourage, we're here to help you
Have a wonderful life and support what you do."

Who helps and guides you on your way?

The Crossroads

You come to a crossroads, a left and a right,
Decisions, decisions, how to choose without fright?
With so many thoughts, with a lot to review,
How to decide on just **what** you should do?

You come to a crossroads, an east and a west,
Life sends you some things that give you a test,
To see what fits you, to give you a choice,
To choose things so wisely, to discover your voice.

You come to a crossroads, a south and a north,
You just can't stand still, you have to go forth.
Remaining there thinking, and life will go by,
Pick one, choose one, you'll just have to try.

You come to a crossroads, an up and a down,
Stay upbeat and open, reject the big frown.
Some things will work out and others will not,
Learn from your options, get going, don't stop.

You come to a crossroads, one for you and for me,
Take **your** own road and see who **you'll** be.
Embrace what you find, make the most of it all,
Meet good and bad times, commit to stand tall.

Smile Wide

Some smiles are large and show big toothy grins.
Some smiles are so big, where **do** they begin?
Some smiles are small and little and cute.
Some smiles are a straight and look like a flute.

Some smiles are round and oval and long.
Some smiles look like you are singing a song.
Some smiles are curved and go ear to ear
Some smiles can say, "I love you my dear."

Be Yourself

Some smiles are sweet, they can make your heart flip.
Some smiles are bold with very broad lips.
Some smiles curl up, they never go down.
Some smiles are wide like you find on a clown.

Some smiles look crooked and a little bit goofy.
Some smiles look like your friend named Ruthy.
Some smiles make you happy, a moment of bliss.
Some smiles look like they are ready to kiss.

Some smiles show you are in a good mood.
Some smiles show you are a really cool dude.
Some smiles show you are **so** very nice.
Some smiles are perfect, they are so precise.

But the best smile there is, and this so is true,
Is the one that **I** have when I spend time with you.

Go share your very best smile!

Make it Better

For years I've heard said, by my dad every day,
"With the start of each morning, it's your Job, capital J,
To notice around you, to improve just **one** thing,
To go make it better—your best you must bring."

Start each **day** with intention, find one thing to improve.
Make at least **one thing** better, now get in your groove
Of doing a bit more, never just getting by,
Of making things better, you can if you try.

Need some ideas? Yeah, I thought that you might.
Just start slow, like when you take a small bite.
Don't go for big, like changing the planet,
Start small like the crystals that shine in black granite.

Be Yourself

It could be the way you play with your brothers,
Or the way you help and talk to your mother.
It could be how you take care of your chores,
Or the way you listen on errands in stores.

It could be the way you are helpful at school,
Or that you never, not ever, act really cruel.
It could be a smile to someone you don't know,
Or helping a neighbor by shoveling their snow.

It could be the way you improve your front yard,
Or the way, with your brother, you don't play really hard.
It could be the way you share your new bike,
Or splitting a snack of the things that you like.

It could be the way you put clean clothes away,
Or the way you help others learn new things each day.
It could be the way you give of your time,
Or hold back for others when it's their turn to climb.

It could be the way you say please and thank you,
Or the way you share some art that you drew.
It could be the way you share all your games,
Or when you feel angry, you act really tame.

In each of the minutes, there's something to do,
That makes the world better, coming from **YOU!**
Find it and do it, pay attention, don't wait,
You'll make a big difference, you'll help life be great.

What is one thing you could make better?

You and Me

You and me, we're just not the same,
You are so wild and I am all tame.
You are so tall and I show up short,
You like all boardgames, I just like sports.

You like all meats and I eat just greens,
You read great books, I like to dream.
Your hair is wavy, straight is what's mine,
Your number is 6, and for me it's a 9.

You like to run, and you love to race,
I like to walk at a much slower pace.
Your music is rap and mine is all rock,
You like to swim; I sit on the dock.

Be Yourself

Your eyes are deep blue; mine are all brown,
You like the city, I love the town.
You are so strong, from time at the gym,
I take long walks, that's how I stay trim.

You love the summer, the heat and the breeze,
I love the fall with the bright-colored leaves.
You love to eat, and I love to cook,
You would not ever be found with a book.

You speak a language that rolls all your r's,
I could spend days just dreaming of cars.
Your skin is dark, mine is much lighter,
You like to paint, and me, I'm a writer.

You like the wind and time with a kite,
I like movies that bring on some fright.
Fancy's your choice, mine is just plain,
You like the sun, but give me the rain.

I see these things that make you **not** me,
So different we are, there just cannot be
One thing that joins us, one thing for us all—
Something that makes us never feel small.

But wait! I see it. It is really bright.
That one thing, that something, that makes us unite.
The more that I watch, pay attention and see,
You are actually **more**, not less, like me.

There **are** many things we all really share,
A need to be loved and a need for great care.
To feel valued and important, to live and let be,
To move through this life and feel really free.

You and Me

Look past the differences that let us be us.
Look past the things that create all the fuss.
Look past the height and look past the weight.
Look past the skin, the hair and those traits.

Go look **IN** others, to see what is great,
The kind heart, the love—see this kind of trait.
Look for the passion, the joy and delight,
Look for their spirit, their inner great light.

See me as different, then see me the same;
Get past my outside, get past my name.
I'm different in things that create all the chatter,
But I **am** just like you for the things that do matter.

So, inside our outsides, we're really alike,
We want the same thing; we want a great life.

**What are some things that make you
different from your friends?**

**What are some things that make you
similar to your friends?**

Learn from
Your World

Look Out Your Window

When its early or late, I can't see outside,
It's dark and that means the outside just hides.

But the moment it's light, great things come in view,
My window shows me the things that are new.

When I look out my window, I see cars drive by,
And with eyes looking up, I see airplanes on high.

When I look out of my window, I see wind in the trees,
The branches all dance as it moves through the leaves.

When I look out of my window, I see rain and some snow,
The cars and the trucks need to go really slow.

When I look out my window, I see people walking,
With arms always moving—they never stop talking.

Learn from Your World

When I look out my window, my neighbors I see,
They always do smile and wave back at me.

When I look out my window, I see kids on the bus,
Laughing and talking with so much to discuss.

When I look out my window, I see men who are mowing,
The yards and the grass that never stop growing.

When I look out my window, I see squirrels and some birds,
They get a lot done without using our words.

When I look out my window, I see big and small dogs,
I see all sorts of bugs and some snakes and some frogs.

When I look out my window, I see flowers so bright,
Red and dark blue, yellow, orange and some white.

When I look out my window, I see people jog,
They run in the rain, in the wind and the fog.

I spend time at my window; I stand still and don't race,
It's my special and very remarkable place.

At my window, I stand and take it all in,
It's how I learn to take life for a spin.

When you stand at your window, what do you see?
What kinds of things make you smile with glee?

Slow Walk

Rush, Rush—go faster and faster,
At this frantic pace, life will be a disaster.
We zoom by all things, with barely a look,
We run fast like police who are chasing a crook.

But what if for once, we could focus on **S L O W**?
Maybe, just maybe, it's a much **better** show.

We **would see** the birds, the bugs and some bees,
We **would see** the flowers, the plants and the trees.

We **would see** our neighbors and have time to say "Hi!"
We wouldn't rush past or hurry right by.

We **would see** the clouds, the rain and the moon,
We **would see** the sun, bright and yellow at noon.

We **would see** our friends and have time to check in,
We'd find out what's doing and where they have been.

We **would see** the new things all around town,
We **would see** things that cheer us when we're down.

A slow walk is something that's **so much** better,
Than even the softness of your favoritest sweater.

Yes, slow is the front seat to life's greatest show,
Slow is my most favorite and best way to go.

Spend time with others, go share in their space,
Slow down, 'cause a **great life** is no kind of race.

How will you slow down today and what could you see?

My Tree All Year

Marcello is a maple tree, in my front yard.
Each day and each night he boldly stands guard.
In the rain and the sun, in the wind and the snow,
Each year he gets grander, we all watch him grow.

In Spring come his leaves with the big warming rain.
I watch as he grows as fast as a train.
First one leaf, then two, then hundreds arrive.
We fertilize and feed him to help him go thrive.

In Summer the sun makes his leaves green and strong.
We play in his shade, **all** the day long.
It's cool and its quiet, under branches so wide.
There in the shade, we count and go hide.

In the Fall comes the wind and his leaves start to change,
From green to some orange and reds, not so strange.
In tumbling leaves we make a great pile,
In it we jump, and we play for a while.

In the Winter that brings the cold and the snow,
On **him** we add lights to put on a show.
He stands **bright and tall** above all the rest,
Dapper and handsome, he's **very** well dressed.

Thank you Marcello, you are family,
The way that you care and watch over me.
In all weathers and seasons, you boldly stand guard,
Protecting and watching right from our front yard.

What trees make your days better?

When the Rain is A-Pouring

From the window I saw, the rain was a-pouring.
My dad on the couch, so loudly a-snoring.
Rainy days—they can seem so a-boring,
That is **until** you go a-exploring.

In my bright yellow coat, I went out in the rain.
The raindrops that fell really banged on my brain.
The ping and pong, the sound was insane,
A feeling that's so very hard to explain.

The rain came down fast, it was heavy and gray.
So, under a tree I thought I would stay,
To watch the rain fall and be out of its way.
But **in** the rain is where **I wanted** to play.

Learn from Your World

I watched falling water go splish and go splash,
Having fun, making puddles, straight down with a crash.
So out in the rain, I ran in a flash,
To add to its splish and to add to its splash.

I danced and I jumped, and I sang really loud,
As the rain kept on falling from one big gray cloud.
The wind moved the branches and together they bowed,
Such great things you see when you're not in a crowd.

The sky was dark, like the color of smoke,
The leaves all danced in our **big** tree—the oak.
The frogs loved the rain, they started to croak,
Rain is such **fun**, that's no lie, no joke.

As I danced and I sang alone in the rain,
Out came my neighbor and bestest friend Jane.
We soared 'round our yards like two crazy planes,
Soaking wet, laughing hard, and loving our games.

But then Jane's mom waved and called her back in,
"Too wet, crazy kids!" But then showed a wide grin.
Yes, we were drenched, soaking wet to our skin,
But what a **great time** it really had been.

I went back in the house; the rain kept a-pouring.
Dad on the couch, with eyes shut and a-snoring.
This rainy day was **so** not a-boring.
Always make time to go a-exploring.

What can you do for fun on a rainy day?

Go Outside

You stayed inside, it's been most of the day,
With bright sun outside, why don't you go play?
Locked onto your tablet, locked on the display,
This is **not good** to be living this way.

Go out and see what the world can show you,
There's many things **old** and many things **new**.
See the trees that are green and the sky that is blue,
There's lots of great stuff for **you** to go do.

Pretend for a moment that the power's all gone,
No lights, no computers for you to turn on.
Go have fun in the woods and on the front lawn,
Go run, invite over, your best buddy Shawn.

Inside the house, it's dark and it's cold,
Go outside and go play before you get old.
For once, please **go do** just as you're told,
You'll find some new treasures even greater than gold.

What great things do you find outside?

The Singing Bell

From a strong branch hung a very small bell,
That sang when the big winds would blow.
At the edge of the woods, across from the dell,
She sang in the sun, rain and snow.

This tiny dear bell, so small and so clear,
Shared her song, her voice, and her tone.
To all who would listen, both far and right near,
When she sang, no one felt alone.

Imagine a life where each day you go sing,
And help others feel **all kinds** of glad.
Sharing your best, your gift or your thing,
To help others be happy, not sad.

So, what gives **you** joy, like the sound of this bell?
What makes your **heart** rise above?
Go and do that, it will help you be well,
And you'll always **share** and **feel** love.

What do you do that makes others feel glad?

The Goose and the Moose

Way deep in the woods, near the edge of a lake,
A goose and a moose, both came face-to-face.
The goose gave a honk and the moose said right back,
"I'm so glad that you honk and do **not** go quack."

The goose said, "I honk, there is no quacking for me,
The ducks own the quacks and I'm glad not to be
A quacker, a yacker, they **just** make such noise,
Like kids on their birthday with many new toys."

"**I** like your honk," the big moose then said,
"It sounds really nice, not something I dread.
Can you honk a bit more, as it sounds oh so sweet?
When I listen to you, it's a wonderful treat."

"Honk, honk," went the goose, who was happy to sing.
The moose hummed along, his voice like a king.
Together they sang, an unusual pair,
Louder and louder without any care.
They sang until dark, when departed the sun.
"Thanks," they each said, "for making the day fun."

Life has surprises, like meeting new folks,
Like smiling and laughing when hearing new jokes.
Watch for the great things that come into view,
And don't be afraid to go try something new.

What is something new you can try?

The Bee and Me

Out in the garden, I decided to go,
I carried my rake and I carried my hoe.
To go spend my time with plants and some flowers.
It's my **favorite** place to spend all my hours.

I **was** not alone, for there was a bee,
Striped black and yellow, flying right next to me.
I smiled and I said, "It's nice to see you.
Fly-hopping on flowers of red, pink and blue."

Buzzing through plants, the mint and the dill.
Then the bee stopped, and became really still.
Looking at him, he was looking at me.
Not afraid in the least, was I of this bee.

Maybe it's true or it's just what I think,
But I thought that I saw him give me a wink.
We spent a nice hour in the garden alone,
And both then decided it's time to go home.

Make time to see nature, it **has** lots to share.
It wants you to walk and spend time with it there.
Go out in the garden, spend time in the trees,
And always remember, be kind to the bees.

How will you make time to be part of nature this week?

Then in no time, a new crossroads you'll meet.
That's life, with great choices, some sour, some sweet.
Meet life where it is, say yes and keep going,
This way you will learn and continue your growing.

What new things do you see today?

The Frog and the Hog

One day at the edge of the pond found these two,
A frog and a hog, face to face, what to do?
They stared at each other, in each their own way,
What then should they do, on this very clear day?

The hog, he just snorted, with a sound really loud.
The frog answered back with a croak, oh so proud.
Both of them laughed, then continued to share,
Loud noises, loud sounds, from each of them there.

Soon others came by to be part of the fun,
With so many sounds that came from each one.

The chirping from birds and the moose's great roar.
The caw of the crow and the grunt of the boar.
The shriek of the eagle, the squeak of the mouse.
The hoot of the owl and the flap of the grouse.
Louder and louder with each passing minute,
The sounds shook the tree and animals in it.

They laughed and they laughed till it got very dark.
One by one, the noisemakers, chose to depart.
Soon the frog and hog were the last to remain,
What fun they both had in their noise-making game.

Great fun is so easy, it just takes some thought.
Make things up, use your mind, and what you've been taught.
Dream big, try new things and go use your voice.
What you do to have fun is always your choice.

How can you have fun today?

The Fawn on the Lawn

On a fog covered morning, to my great surprise,
I was greeted by two of the largest brown eyes.
They came with a tiny and chestnut soft face,
That stood near the woods with a heavenly grace.

From out of the trees came a bright little fawn,
Who marched forth with courage, right onto my lawn.
No fear, just some interest, to see about me,
While I sat on my deck with a hot cup of tea.

"Welcome sweet fawn," I smiled as I said,
"There's lots to eat here, and there's **nothing** to dread.
I love that you come and feel safe in my yard.
As you eat and you roam, I'll **always** stand guard."

"You are **safe** little one," I said to the fawn,
"To come and spend time right here on my lawn.
Come back any day, with the bugs and the birds,
My smile I will give, and my gentle soft words."

It's important in life to have your own space,
Where you're loved and respected and feel very safe.
To spend time with others, who openly care,
With time and attention, they're willing to share.

Be happy little one, find joy in this life.
My wish that's for you is for days without strife.
Enjoy life and frolic, and try some things new,
Have fun, but stay close, to those who love you.

Who are some of the people who love you?

A Fish with Four Eyes

Maybe you know this, and maybe you don't,
There's a fish with four yellow eyes.
Who lives **deep** in the ocean, that's dark with no motion,
And eats yummy green seaweed pies.

Now I know you may ask, what is the need,
For a fish with so many eyes?
But down deep it's so dark, with no light or no spark,
Four eyes can find seaweed pies.

What's one thing that makes you special?

The Skunk in a Funk

Deep in the woods, far from the houses,
Lived a family of deer with the last name—the Rouses.
Along with the deer lived a large moose named Sigg,
Who was broad and was strong and was wonderfully big.

In those same woods, lived Theo the skunk.
Though handsome, he spent all his time in a funk.
See, he noticed the gifts that all others had,
But he, and they knew it, just smelled really bad.

The deer and the moose all held
their long noses,
And cried as he passed,
"He's no bed of roses."
The laughed and they teased and
all called him names.
It's hard to be happy when you feel
so ashamed.

The Skunk in a Funk

The deer shook their legs and their little white tails,
Saying, "We run so fast and don't leave a trail."
They showed off their gift of super great speeds,
Through woods and the meadow and in between trees.

The big moose just laughed and then nodded his head,
"Yes, you run fast," he knowingly said,
"But I'm strong and tall, and can eat from a tree.
No one is stronger or bolder than me."

Then turning to Theo, the moose said "Please tell,
What can **you** do but make the air smell?"
They laughed and they laughed with such a great sound,
That it shaked and it shooked the woods and the ground.

"No wonder I always seem in a funk."
Thought Theo, feeling sad for being a skunk.
"They think they are funny when **they** say these things.
Their words really hurt; their words really sting."

So, Theo moved off to a more private spot,
Feeling hurt and so down that **this** was his lot.
To be stinky and smelly, and always be sad,
Why do his friends always make him feel bad?

Alone and dejected he sat on the ground,
But then quickly noticed someone was around.
A hunter, no, three, were now in the woods,
A cause for alarm, so near where he stood.

The family of deer and Sigg the big moose,
Came into the clearing, right by the blue spruce.
They laughed and they played, not knowing the dangers,
Brought into the woods by these scary strangers.

Learn from Your World

What now could **he** do, this fragrant black skunk,
Who always was so very deep in a funk?
But friends are in trouble, he knew it right then,
He had to protect them from these three tall men.

The skunk took a breath and went out where it's clear,
Headed straight for the hunters, without any fear.
He got close, he turned, and then started to spray.
Not one of those hunters decided to stay.

Seeing the hunters go run for the hills,
Aware of the danger, gave the animals chills.
They'd been **so** busy playing and were not aware,
Of the danger and peril going on right there.

The Skunk in a Funk

They went up to Theo, with "Thank-You"s so keen,
And said they were sorry for acting so mean.
His courage had saved them by using his smell,
He cared and he shared, with the thing he does well.

Theo smiled, then looked deep into their eyes,
He could have been mad, but instead he was wise.
"We each have our own gifts," he said to each mate.
"Mine are not yours, but mine are still great."

"We're **not** all the same, that **may** be the plan,
We do what we must, and then do what we can."
Said Theo, "I hope you will never lament
That what I do best is the use of a scent."

From that day on—the bad talk—it all ended,
Accepted he was, and it surely felt splendid.
We each have our thing; he got rid of his funk,
His gifts are courage and the smell of a skunk.

What are some of your greatest gifts?

To Laugh
and Have Fun

The Wiggles and Giggles

Sitting in church or at my school desk,
I seem to always go wiggle.
My feet and my bum **cannot** stay still,
What happens next is I **giggle**.

I wiggle and giggle nonstop,
Soon **all** of my friends do the same.
The wiggly giggles are endless,
We roll on the floor with no shame.

"Stop this right now!" the adults do say,
"Act your age, we're talking to you!"
We try to stop, we try to get calm,
But then **they** start giggling too.

When giggling starts, no one is mad,
It makes us **all** start to grin.
No matter the place, we all feel so glad,
We can't help but want to join in.

Sherry LaShot

Let me tell you about Miss Sherry LaShot,
Whose nose was always so filled with snot.
"Blow your nose," said her mom, "because you just ought
To get all that out or it's going to rot."

But Sherry just made a **big** episode,
Of not wanting to clear out her nose of the load.
Said her mom with a frown, "Live with this code:
If you don't blow your nose, your head will explode."

Pa-Duddles

You say puddles and I say pa-duddles,
It's just so much **more fun** to say.
You then say splash and I say spla-tash
I say these when skies are all gray.

I like to jump in the biggest pa-duddles,
With water all over my laces.
I spla-tish over here and spla-tash over there,
Sending water all over the places.

Tony Spumoni

Down the street lives the big brood Spumoni,
All ten of their kids are named Tony.
Each son is real strong and not boney.
Their house is so sturdy and stoney.

It's true, they share the same name,
The parents hoped it would bring them some fame.
But when they called, all ten of them came.
Good thing all ten kids do **not** look the same.

Ten kids, you might ask me, how **much** do they eat?
Big mountains of pasta and plenty of meat.
Now, Mama Spumoni, so kind and so sweet,
Makes sure that each Tony has his own treat.

The Box

It's been sitting there now most of the day,
Delivered this morning, my mother did say.
"It's **not** for you, but your big brother Ray.
Don't touch it, just leave it, just let it stay."

But I find that I **can't** just go with the flow.
What's in this big box, the color of snow?
Could it be games or even something to grow?
If **I** could just peek, then **no one** will know.

I open the top, now what do I see?
Blue gitter is everywhere, blowing so free.
Now covered in glitter, to an epic degree.
My big brother played a great joke on me.

Mom crossed her arms and was mad as you'd guess.
I feared this would bring a really big stress.
She just shook her head, then calmly said, "Yes.
I hope that you've learned, now clean up this mess."

My Snake Named Jake

My name is Jake and my snake's name is Jake,
I **bet** you think this is strange.
But I love the name Jake and love having a snake,
So, I thought I should use the same name.

My snake named Jake, I found in a lake,
The one at the end of our street.
My pet named Jake is a helpful green snake,
At home he helps me stay neat.

My snake named Jake, he loves to create,
He's so smart—he knows how to read.
This snake named Jake, no fuss does he make,
Reading books at a **very** fast speed.

My Snake Named Jake

My snake named Jake, he really can bake,
He knows how to stir and to blend.
I call him chef Jake, he makes the best cakes,
For me and for all of my friends.

My happy pet snake, the one I call Jake,
Follows wherever I go.
He's more than a snake, a great friend he does make,
Together we go to and fro.

You'd want a snake, like the one **I** named Jake,
As a friend, he's loyal and strong.
A snake like Jake, good times he will make,
You'll have fun when you bring him along.

Neil McNutter and His Butter

Here is the story of big Neil McNutter,
Who lived in a house with a great deal of clutter.
He spent all his days making bluish nut butter.
The mere **look** of it made **all** his friends shudder.

"But try it," insisted kind Neil McNutter.
"I promise it'll make your hearts go a-flutter."
They all then tasted, and soon they all did utter,
"We **do** truly love McNutter nut butter."

I Smell

I smell, yes I do, with my very big nose.
It sticks out ahead, like some carnival shows.
It can smell highs; it can also smell lows.
In the winter it gets all icy and froze.

My nose can discover the things that are sweet.
It can tell if something is bad or a treat.
It knows when it's time to go clean my feet.
It knows if we're having pie or some meat.

Be friends with your nose, it's one of your kin.
If long or pointed or even real thin.
Maybe it's thick or way down to your chin,
Or flat and real wide like a metal dustbin.

My nose helps me find my way every day.
It can give me a warning to go or to stay.
It can tell if the weather is bright or is gray.
My nose is my friend and I like it that way.

Grayson McFees

I wonder if you know my friend Grayson McFees,
Whose favorite thing was to spend time up in trees.
He'd climb way on up just to be in the breeze.
He spent all his time in the branches and leaves.

So much time he did spend, way up in the trees,
It took a big toll on that Grayson McFees.
Turned into a monkey and swung through the leaves,
From branch to branch with his face in the breeze.

Now **don't** be all worried, I'll put you at ease,
In the trees with the breeze, so happy was heez.

Along the Bumpy Road

Mary Simoes and Her Clothes

Mary Simoes, just loved to buy clothes,
She always dressed well and dressed smart.
With fashions for all of life's highs and its lows,
She wore clothes that showed her big heart.

See, all the clothes of Mary Simoes,
Were always in some shade of red.
Covered was she from her nose to her toes,
"I **only** wear red," she then said.

Mary Simoes, who loved all her clothes,
One day, she fell into a stream.
Wet were her clothes from her toes to her nose,
Now **all** had become a bright green.

With a shriek and pout, she stumbled right out,
Of that water that's not very clean.
"The red's all gone out!" Mary did shout,
Then smiled at her **green** clothes, so keen.

Now as it goes, our Mary Simoes,
Adds in pinks and yellows and blues.
From **that** day she chose, to buy all her clothes,
In many more colors and hues.

About the Author

Passionate to help others discover, develop and live what is best in them, to be ready for great and amazing lives, Jay Forte, a certified executive coach, educator, author and family poet, shares important life lessons in all he writes.

Growing up in a large Italian family, raising three daughters, actively engaging with eight grandchildren and supporting organizations and dynamic workplaces, have provided Jay with endless wisdom and humor that inspires his stories and poems. Life is truly a comedian and our best teacher—we must laugh as we learn each day.

Jay has created the "Let's Activity Together" series, a collection of interactive activity books, and the "Let's Read Together" series, a collection of interactive stories and poems, to help families imagine, create, communicate and spend time together, away from technology. Jay is also the author of numerous poetry books and **The Greatness Zone—Know Yourself, Find Your Fit, Transform the World**, an important life resource to teach everyone how to find their place in today's world.

Passionate about words and rhyme, his work has been called "profound, funny, entertaining and wise—a modern poet." And, as a caring coach, dad and grampie, he always encourages kids and parents to expand their creativity, imagination, focus on adventure and personal contribution.

When not helping people to be their best, build stronger family bonds, solve challenges and learn how to do their part to make a better world, Jay writes, gardens and cooks, spending time with his big family in both New England and the Florida Keys.

To see more of Jay's family and children-based books, collections and resources, go to TheGreatnessZone.com

About the Illustrator

James Monroe is an experienced illustrator and graphic designer with over 18 years of expertise in creating captivating visuals for books, collaborating closely with authors and publishers to bring their stories to life. Known for his versatile style and keen eye for detail, James has developed a reputation for his ability to seamlessly blend traditional and digital techniques, crafting illustrations that resonate with audiences of all ages. His portfolio includes a diverse range of projects, from children's books to complex graphic novels, showcasing his talent for storytelling through art. Passionate about visual communication, James is dedicated to enhancing narratives with his unique artistic vision, making him a sought-after professional in the publishing industry.

Please visit jamesmonroedesign.com

The Books of Wisdom/Work

Wisdom/Work is a new cooperative, cutting edge imprint and resource for publishing and offering books by practical philosophers and innovative thinkers that provide a positive cultural impact, the best of ancient and modern wisdom with guidance for all to be ready for life at every stage. When we do the inner wisdom work, it elevates our experience.

A primary focus of the Wisdom/Work imprint is to make available high-quality content with expedited production and release and expanded benefits to authors, filling the broad publication gap between the scholarly world of university press books that are focused on academic concerns and the fast-paced world of major trade publishers, focused mainly on profit. By encouraging and supporting authors to develop and share practical wisdom for all ages and stages of life around the themes of success, ethics, happiness, meaning, purpose, partnership, the nature of good work, the many shapes of fulfilling adventure, and how best to live a good life in our time, the Wisdom/Work imprint provides a greater reader experience, practical life-success wisdom, and affordability for book buyers.

The imprints of Wisdom/Work and The Greatness Zone work in partnership to provide engaging, informative, and practical wisdom-based books for today's younger audiences and families.

For inquiries into our current and future publishing plans, to become acquainted with all Wisdom/Work books or to purchase books at a bulk discount, please inquire through the website of the founder and editor in chief, Tom Morris, TomVMorris.com. For more information about the books of The Greatness Zone, see TheGreatnessZone.com.

Made in the USA
Columbia, SC
13 October 2024

c8a29ae4-9692-41bf-8a8e-0122b7d2b314R01